MY SPECIAL HEART

I have a special heart,
that has two valves and not three.
My mom and dad were scared, but no not me!

The valves pump blood to and from the heart.
The heart uses the blood to give the body a jump start.

MY SPECIAL HEART

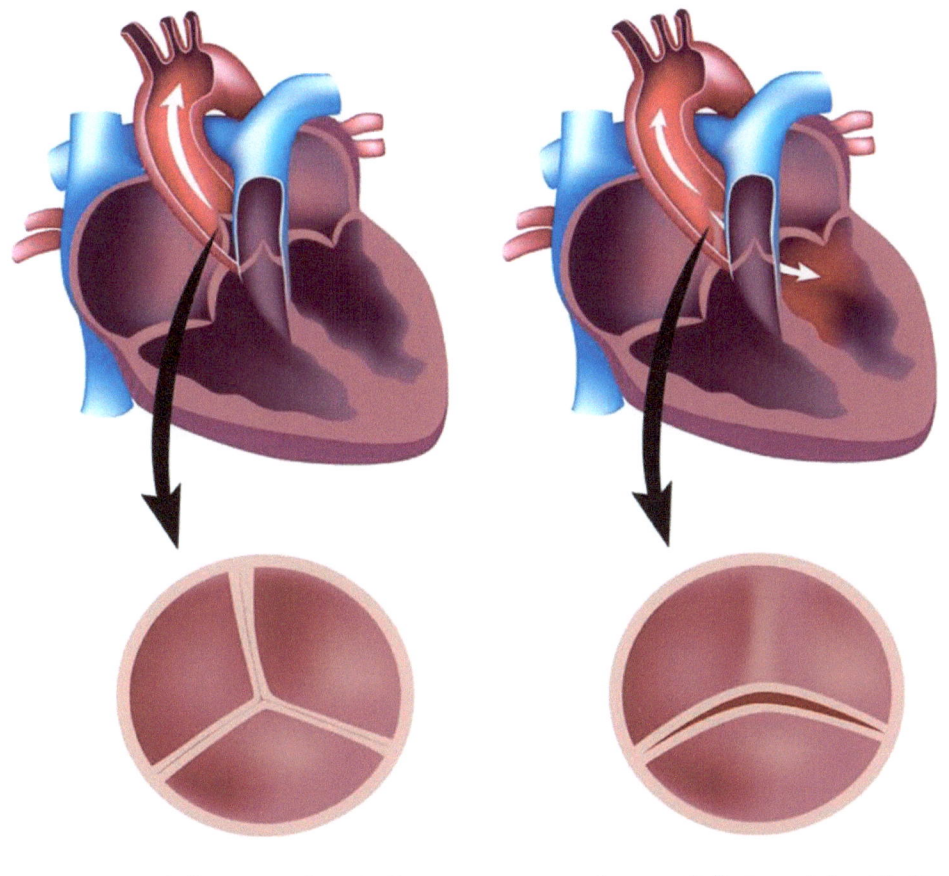

Tricuspid Aortic Valve

(Your heart looks like this)

Bicuspid Aortic Valve

(My heart looks like this)

MY SPECIAL HEART

My heart works extra hard, like my mom does every day.

One day it could get tired and make me feel a different kind of way.

MY SPECIAL HEART

Once or twice a year I see a doctor called a
CAR-DI-OL-O-GIST.
This is a very important visit that I can never miss.

**MY SPECIAL HEART**

My mom is always there to hold me and the doctor is really nice.

But I get a little concerned when they turn off all the lights.

MY SPECIAL HEART

I
get
really
REALLY scared.....

08

MY SPECIAL HEART

A nurse tells me to lay down, as if I'm taking a rest.
She puts these little stickers all over my chest.

I feel like I'm being attacked! By an octopus,
with all its little feet.

E ach sticker has a sensor,
that draws lines that match my heart beat.

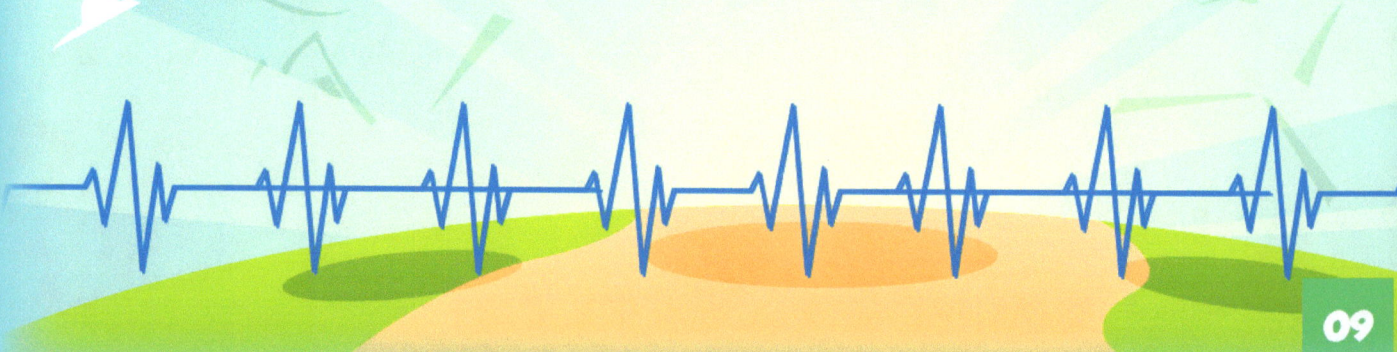

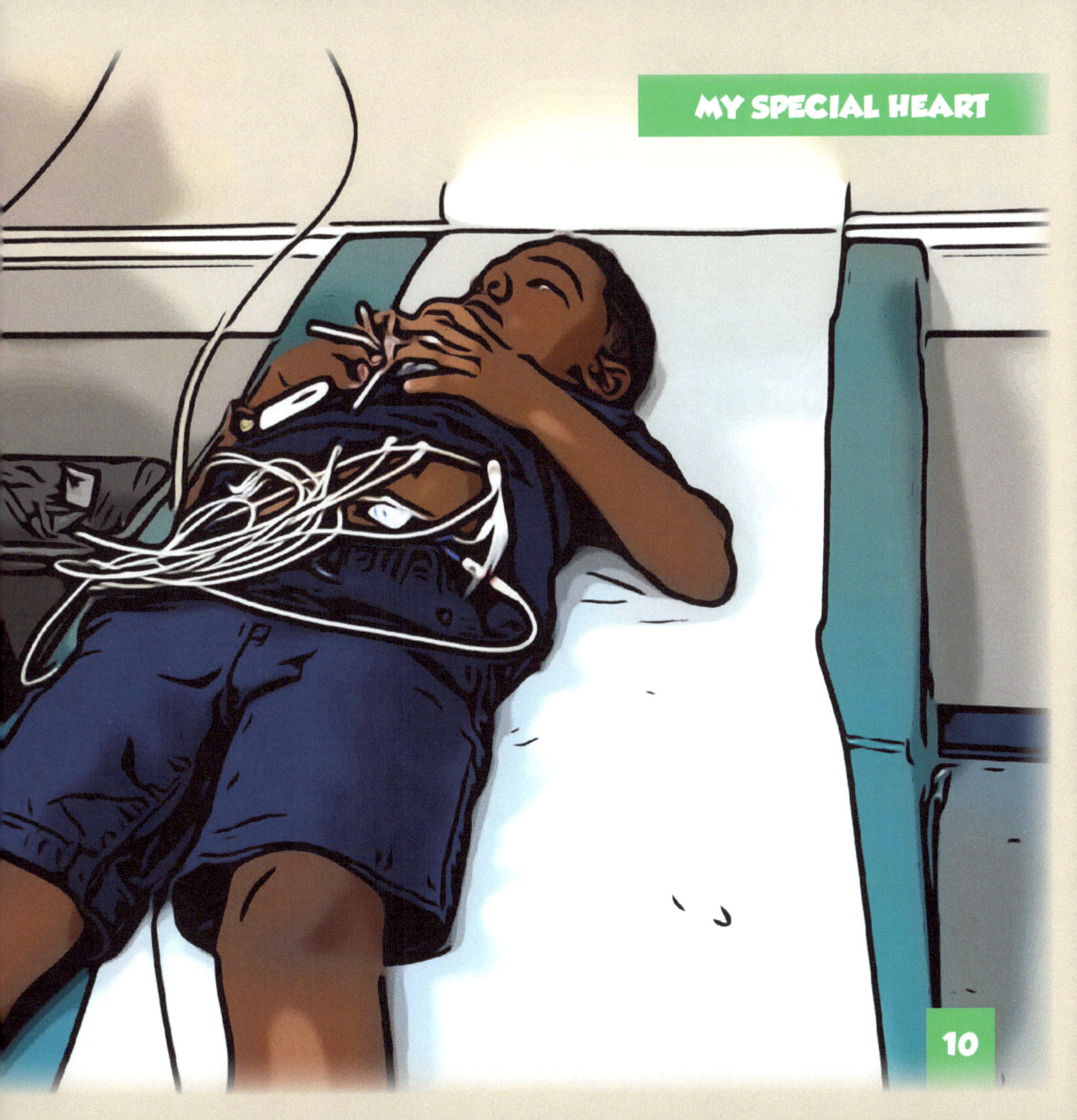

MY SPECIAL HEART

The doctor then rubs a special gel all over my chest.
Using his magical wand he makes a huge mess!

It all feels pretty weird!
Especially, since I was scared from the start.

But then it all becomes super **cool**,
when I see the pictures and live video of my special heart.

MY SPECIAL HEART

The Doctor usually says he's happy that I came.

Although my heart is different from most, it is working just the same.

MY SPECIAL HEART

I can do everything that all my friends could.
I eat extra fruits and vegetables like a healthy kid should.

MY SPECIAL HEART

I brush my teeth a little longer and after every meal.

My dentist already told me that cavities are a bad deal.

MY SPECIAL HEART

I run and jump and play,
but sometimes i have to take rest.

I listen to my body
and I always try my best.

MY SPECIAL HEART

None of my friends know about
My Special Heart.
But teaching them about it, is a great start.

MY SPECIAL HEART

I have a special heart that I wanted to **share with you.** I hope one day to hear about all the things that make you special too.

www.ingramcontent.com/pod-product-compliance
Lightning Source LLC
Chambersburg PA
CBHW041408160426
42811CB00106B/1558